Oil & The Global Capitalist Crisis

Presentation by Caleb Maupin to the Second Congress of the Trade Union Center of Brazil on February 25th, 2016

Caleb Maupin

Caleb T. Maupin
Copyright © 2016 Caleb Maupin

Cover Design: Ramiro Funez

Presentation given by Caleb Maupin at the Second Congress of the Trade Union Center of Brazil (CSB) on February 25, 2016 in Brasilia.

It such a deep honor to be here in Brazil, at a conference of labor leaders.

I've always had the utmost respect and admiration for organized labor.

I know that I'm looking out into an audience of brilliant minds, experts, people who are very skilled, and who have carefully refined the art of organizing the working people of Brazil to fight for justice.

I'm invited here today, from what I understand, because of my expertise in the field of economics and politics. I'm going to speak about the global economy, the price of oil, and what can be done. I thank you for the invitation.

I want people to sit back in your seat, relax, and get comfortable. Take a few deep breaths. I'm going to hit you with a lot of information in the next hour and a half, but I think it will clarify a lot of things.

I know there are a lot of things going on in Brazilian politics which are directly linked to oil. I'm not going to directly comment on these things. I'm going to talk about the global economy, and put everything in context.

Oil Bankers: The Richest People in the World

Who is the richest person in the world? The international media often tries to answer that question for us. Names get floated around like Bill Gates, Carlos Slim, Warren Buffet -- sometimes they'll mention an Arab sultan or prince. Forbes magazine publishes a list of the richest people in the world.

All of this utter nonsense.

Bill Gates, Carlos Slim, Warren Buffet, the king of Saudi Arabia, all of these people are poor men compared to the ones who have real power. These people are listed as the richest people in the world, because they are so poor, that they have all of their money listed in their own name.

Those who are really rich, those with the most wealth, power and influence, have astronomical amounts of wealth, often so much money that their total net worth cannot even be calculated.

The richest people in the world can be described in two words: oil bankers.

The House of Rockefeller, the House of Morgan, the Carnegies, the Rothschilds, the Mellons, the Du Ponts -- these oil and banking dynasties sit at the center of a small network of deeply entrenched power and influence, dominating the economies of the United States and western Europe, and most of the rest of the planet.

Let's take the most powerful family of oil bankers, the Rockefellers, as a case study.

When Nelson Rockefeller, one of the many heirs of John D. Rockefeller and the Standard Oil cartel of the 1880s, was being questioned by the US Congress in 1974, some of the most brilliant investigative reporters, journalists, and economists assembled to cover the hearing.

Among them, none of them could determine exactly how much money Nelson Rockefeller really had.

In his own name, Mr. Rockefeller personally had a few billion dollars. The rest of his money was tied up in an elaborate network -- thousands of trusts, small corporations, and foundations he controlled.

When testifying before Congress, Nelson Rockefeller was asked about his control of Chase Manhattan Bank. He testified, honestly, "I don't own a single share of Chase Manhattan Bank." He was telling the truth. He personally did not have a single cent invested in Chase. However, one of the trusts he controlled owned well over 325,000 shares of stock in Chase Manhattan Bank.

That was back in the 1970s. Today the wealth and influence of one of two most powerful oil-banking cliques is combined. The House of Rockefeller holds control of the largest super-major oil company, Exxon-Mobil, as its personal property. In addition, this powerful family jointly controls an entity called JP Morgan-Chase with the Morgans, another powerful family in the United States. JP Morgan Chase is the largest banking entity in the entire world.

The Morgans, now partnered with the Rockefellers, are descendants of an infamous Wall Street legend named JP Morgan. Not only the Rockefellers and

Morgans control JP Morgan Chase, they also control a company called General Electric, the sixth-largest firm in the United States.

There is no key aspect of the global economy that the old bankers haven't put their stamp on, and tried very hard to craft in their own interest. General Electric ranks 21st among corporations contracted by the US military. This entity controlled by the Rockefellers and Morgans has over 6,674 contracts with the Pentagon, bringing in over $2 billion a year in US military projects alone. You can be sure that the US military brass is very concerned about making sure that the Rockefellers and the Morgans are happy with whatever decision they make.

Furthermore, a global media conglomerate called NBC Universal, which includes MSNBC and Comcast, is owned controlled by General Electric.

Universal Studios, one of the "big six" in Hollywood, is also their property as well.

Most art museums in the United States are directly linked to Rockefeller foundations, if not directly controlled by them. Like the Museum of Modern Art in New York City, without the direct approval of the Rockefellers, we may never have known the names Andy Warhol or Jackson Pollock.

Almost every major college and university in the United States depends on money from Rockefeller-controlled foundations, a relationship that puts academia under the direct control of the oil bankers.

More interestingly, the US Central Intelligence Agency crafts its policies and conducts its research with a private foundation called the Council on Foreign Relations. Exxon-Mobil and variety of Rockefeller Foundations, along with the Ford Foundation, completely bankroll this powerful institution of academics and former US elected officials.

The Council on Foreign Relations, controlled by oil bankers, is essentially the brain of the CIA. The smartest minds in the United States are paid six-figure salaries to carefully make proposals and calculations about how the United States should wield its influence around the world. Put simply, the Council on Foreign Relations thinks it up, but the CIA does it.

And even the manner in which the CIA operates around the world is directly accountable to the Rockefeller, Morgan, and Ford dynasties. The CIA does very little work on its own. CIA agents aren't generally the ones getting their hands dirty, conducting military coups, kidnapping people, torturing people, etc.

The CIA generally has the job of finding dupes and allies in the country of interest, instructing them, advising them, and letting them carry out the tasks that serve US foreign policy interest. The key way for the CIA to help those doing its dirty work around the world is connecting them to Wall Street-controlled non-governmental organizations and foundations.

The CIA goes into a country. It finds people to carry out its mission, and then the network of wealthy families that control Exxon-Mobil, Chevron, British Petroleum, and Royal Dutch Shell pay them for it.

The National Endowment for Democracy, the Open Society Institute -- the whole network of activist groups controlled by George Soros -- fund the activities of the CIA's allies, dupes, and collaborators in almost every corner of the globe.

You can find the money of the wealthy oil banking families in the United States all over the world, and often on multiple sides of different political issues. The oil banking dynasties, working with the CIA and the Pentagon, use their funding and money like an expert sports gambler. If you put money on both teams, you are guaranteed to win almost every game.

Every country in the world has money from the oil bankers somehow manipulating its political process. Organizations that say they advocate "democracy," "human rights," "economic freedom," and "social justice" are getting money from the big oil bankers and getting instructions from the CIA.

If you want to find the people who run the world, the quietly powerful global elite, you don't have to look for the Illuminati, the Freemasons, or some secret society. Look at the major oil companies and banks in the United States and Western Europe and the families whose money is historically tied up in them.

The four major oil corporations in the United States, the "super-majors" as they are called -- Chevron, British Petroleum, the Rothschilds' Royal Dutch Shell, and the Rockefellers' Exxon-Mobile -- don't really compete with each other. They function as much like a trust or cartel as is legally possible in the United States. They set the prices of gasoline together. They discuss increases and drops in production among each other.

A number of smaller corporations, which are indirectly owned by the same people that own the Big Four, follow right behind them. An oil company called Marathon is technically an independent company, but it's really just a subdivision of Exxon-Mobil, another descendant of Standard Oil. It's technically a competitor with the Big Four, but this only true on paper.

US foreign policy cannot be separated from the power of oil corporations. This should be obvious from a distance. What countries have been the biggest enemies and military opponents of the United States in the last three decades? Iraq, Libya, Venezuela, Russia, Iran. All of these countries are major oil exporters.

And who pays for the Council on Foreign Relations? Who does business with the Pentagon? Who owns the banks at the center of the European Union? Who funds both the Democratic and Republican Parties in the United States? Who funds the Labour Party, the Conservative Party, and the Liberal Democratic Party in Britain?

The very ground on which the United Nations Headquarters in Manhattan was constructed was a personal donation from the Rockefeller family.

Henry Kissinger, one of the leading influential figures in setting US foreign policy, is a complete creation of the oil bankers. He worked for the Rockefellers before he worked in Washington.

If you look at the think tanks where decisions are made by powerful leaders, you'll see that roughly the same people work at them and the same people fund them. The Asia Society, the Brookings Institute, the American Enterprise Institute, the Hoover Institution, the Heritage Foundation; it's not hard to find out where all of these policy-setting institutions get their money. You can always trace it back to oil bankers.

So with that in mind, I am going to answer the following questions:

So, why did the oil-price drop in 2014? Why does it remain below $30 per barrel? What is the relationship between oil and development? Why is the global economy facing a crisis?

The Fruits of High Oil

Let's go back to the first year of the 21st century. Following 2001, the policies crafted by the Council on Foreign Relations and carried out by US president Bush and Tony Blair in Britain had one obvious impact: they drove oil prices up.

When Iraq was invaded on March 19th, 2003, the US military destroyed the country's infrastructure with a cruise missile torrent known as "shock and awe." Iraq was one of the leading oil producers in the world. It was removed from the world market. Millions of Iraqis died.

The price of oil went up.

Almost immediately after Iraq was destroyed, the US, Britain, and Israel began to escalate an international campaign against one of Iraq's neighbors and one of Saddam Hussein's biggest enemies: the Islamic Republic of Iran. A barrage of media propaganda insinuated that Iran was trying to build nuclear weapons, and the international community was rallied to put sanctions on Iran. The sanctions restricted Iran's ability to export.

The price of oil got even higher.

In 2008, the US-aligned regime in Georgia attacked the Russian-aligned territories of South Ossetia. Georgia is a country that is completely aligned with the United States. It purchases military hardware exclusively from the United States. US-NATO troops are stationed in the country.

Georgia attacked South Ossetia, which Russia was obligated to protect. In response, Russia and Georgia had a war.

In response, sanctions were placed on Russia, restricting its right to export oil on the international markets.

As Bush left office in January 2009, the oil prices had reached the highest levels in world history: over $110 per barrel.

The four super-majors were making record profits.

The Council on Foreign Relations, the Pentagon, the CIA, all directly linked and accountable to the four super-major oil companies, had carried out a series of policies that resulted in astronomically high profits for the four super-major oil companies.

This cannot be dismissed as merely a coincidence.

However, in the process of engineering US foreign policy toward making astronomical profits, the four super-majors created major problems on the international markets.

The Bolivarian government of Venezuela uses proceeds from the state owned oil corporation to subsidize low income housing and other social programs.

In Venezuela, Chavez took office in 1999, and enacted a new constitution. He beat back the 2002 coup d'état against him, due to his popularity with rank-and-file soldiers.

In 2003, as oil prices were rising, Chavez drastically altered the nature of the Venezuelan nationalized oil resources. He reoriented Venezuela's oil so that the proceeds would go almost entirely into the domestic budget.

Chavez became amazingly popular as he provided free healthcare, free education, and other services to the population in Venezuela. Chavez and the United Socialist Party set up an oil-funded apparatus of activists. Venezuela became an opponent of the United States on the global stage, as the Venezuelan state got stronger due to the high oil prices.

Russia got stronger also. During the 1990s, in the aftermath of the collapse of the Soviet Union, Russia was an economic disaster. Massive unemployment, massive crime. The country depopulated as people fled in order to survive.

But with the oil boom, Vladimir Putin was able to restart the Russian economy. The Putin government was able to put Russia back into order by exporting oil and natural gas, and funding a strong state apparatus in the process.

The booming oil prices enabled Putin to launch his National Priorities Project, vastly improving the state-run health service, subsidizing housing for low-income Russians, and creating an anti-imperialist media.

With state-controlled petroleum and natural gas, the industrial output increased by 125%. The rate of industrial expansion was 70%. The wages of Russian workers tripled during the first eight years of the Putin Administration. Between 2007 and 2014, the Russian gross domestic product increased from $764 billion to $2,096.8 billion.

The Russian state became a force to be reckoned with once again.

Summer camps for academically high-achieving youth were created, as part of the youth organization called "Nashi." At the summer camps, the youth of Russia who are deemed to have the most potential are urged to use their skills to advance the Russian nation, not to get rich.

The Russian state aligned with the Russian Orthodox Church to forge a new ideology, a kind of anti-capitalist Christian Russian nationalism. The Russian state apparatus is influenced by the legacy of the Soviet Union, and takes pride in the defeat of Adolph Hitler. People around the world call this the "New Russian Patriotism." The slogan that Putin rallied his supporters around in 2008 was "Together We Win." He urged Russians to reject the western concepts of individualism and selfishness, and be part of a collective effort to build a strong country.

In the Islamic Republic of Iran, the high oil prices strengthened the figures in Iranian politics who call themselves "Principalists," though they are derogatorily called "hardliners" in western media. The hostility from the United States, who dubbed Iran part of the "axis of evil," combined with the high oil prices to give a huge boost to the ideological organizations that serve as the backbone of the Islamic Republic.

The Islamic Revolutionary Guard Corps, the Basigue, the Islamic University system, the forces that emphasize the anti-capitalist goals of the 1979 revolution, all found themselves with lots of money. Ahmadinejad implemented a number of domestic reforms that built up the Iranian countryside, funded public works projects for Iranian workers, and strengthened Iranian labor unions.

While Chevron, British Petroleum, Royal Dutch Shell, and Exxon-Mobil were making record profits, their hired analysts were warning them that the world was slipping out of their fingers. In the post-Cold War era, suddenly a new opposition was on the scene.

Beyond Russia, Venezuela, and Iran, the Islamic socialist government of Libya grew more powerful due to the oil-price increase. Colonel Muammar Gaddafi was elected President of the African Union.

Ecuador saw significant economic growth, recovering from the horrors of neoliberalism in the 1990s.

Here in Brazil, your government-controlled oil company Petrobas became the third-largest corporation in the hemisphere. Petrobas, an oil company that is not controlled by the Big Four oil corporations, with the majority of the shares owned by your popularly elected government, was larger than BP, larger than Exxon-Mobile, even larger than Microsoft.

In the parts of the world where oil is not controlled by Wall Street bankers, but controlled by popular governments, the high oil prices, inflated by US foreign policy, gave a huge boost to the living conditions of the people. People in Brazil, Russia, Venezuela, Ecuador, Iran, and Libya saw their lives getting better.

The Koch-Fracker Insurgency

And not only on the global stage did a new slew of opponents and competitors arise. Within the United States, suddenly you had a surge of financial power flowing into the hands of independent oil and natural gas companies. The Big Four oil companies can be called "big oil," but the high oil prices and breakthroughs in technological development empowered "little oil" to be stronger than ever.

Hydraulic fracking became legal and widespread. Fracking is a practice in which boiling steam is used to extract subterranean oil and natural gas. Fracking opened up deposits of petroleum and natural gas found in the shale, the rock layer that is below the soil. Because of this technological innovation, a whole slew of tiny, unknown oil corporations suddenly emerged to challenge the monopoly of the Big Four.

Because of fracking, the United States is now the top oil and natural gas producer in the world. The 1973 oil-export ban, imposed because of the OPEC boycott, has been lifted. US oil companies can now export on the international markets.

A number of small energy corporations, who previously had almost been irrelevant, suddenly made billions of dollars. Devon Energy, a tiny energy firm based in Oklahoma, was suddenly rising up to power on the stock market. Cenovus Energy, a Canadian energy producer, pops up and starts extracting from Canada's tar sands.

Throughout the first decade of the 21st century, US domestic oil production is rising, and with it astronomically high energy prices. Not only are the Big Four making record profits, but these "little oil men," a crowd of swamp speculators and low-level capitalists, also made billions of dollars.

Exxon-Mobil, the Council on Foreign Relations, and the entrenched, old-money oil bankers began to move into the Democratic Party by 2007 and 2008. This is a rational decision for anyone who closely follows US politics. The demographics of US society are shifting.

The white middle class elderly FOX news viewers, the traditional base of social conservatism, is dying off. A much larger percentage of the US public is Black or Latino. Young whites also vote for

Democrats and have liberal views, especially on social issues. The Republican base of white, conservative, nationalistic middle class Christians -- the backbone of Nixon, Reagan, and Bush -- is dying off. The propaganda style crafted by the neoconservatives is not effective any longer.

As Big Oil moved out of the Republicans, the frackers and new oil opposition moved in.

Big Oil is sophisticated in its politics. It has huge think tanks, studying trends in global economics and politics, figuring out carefully how to secure its power for the long term.

But "little oil" isn't so sophisticated. Sarah Palin, the governor of Alaska, who had long been a champion of the little oil men, was nominated as the vice presidential candidate for the Republican Party in 2008. Her base is "little oil." One of her campaign slogans was "Drill, baby, drill!"

What she was really saying was, "Open up Alaska to the small oil corporations." She brags that she fought against "Big Oil" as governor of Alaska, and there's a little bit of truth in it. Palin's husband wasn't even a registered Republican for many years. For a long time he was aligned with the Alaskan State

Independence Party, the John Birch Society, and the Constitution Party.

The politics overtaking the Republican Party in the aftermath of the Bush Administration is not the pragmatic neoconservatism crafted carefully by Exxon-Mobil in the 70s and 80s. It is ideological right-wing paleo-conservatism. These are individuals who think the United States is run by a secret conspiracy of communists. These are individuals who think the public educational system is a plot to wipe out Christianity. These are the forces who were driven out of the Republican Party in the early 1960s, after they said that Dwight D. Eisenhower was a communist. These are the individuals who say Abraham Lincoln was a dictator, and that the slave-owners of the US south were justified in taking up arms against the republic.

The new oil money has turned the weakened and isolated Republican Party into a platform to fight against the Big Four oil corporations and their near monopoly on US oil profits. Unlike the Rockefellers, who have learned to use the government to secure their power, they call for "laissez faire," "hands-off" economics. They believe if everything were privatized, everyone could be rich like them.

The billionaires of new oil money see themselves caught between two great chasms. On the one hand, they are opposing the big oil bankers who want to drive them off the market. However, they are just as threatened, if not more threatened, by the global anti-capitalist movements. The labor unions, the Occupy Wall Street protests, the mass movements for social justice -- all represent the threat that their wealth could be redistributed.

They see the rising social movements against capitalism as a heartless mob, people they deem to be inferior assembling to crush them. They see in the Big Oil capitalists a group of monopolists who want to smash their independence and absorb them into the collective.

The only place they can look for consolation is the past. They call for a "new 1776." They dream of "restoring the republic" with some kind of bloody purge.

Some people call these politics emanating from new money in the Republican Party fascism. I don't know if this is accurate.

The Democratic Party hates two men in particular who have become the symbolic leaders of the fracking new oil insurgency. These two oil billionaires, Charles and David Koch, the inheritors of an oil company called "Koch Industries," have become the target of scorn by the voices of the Democratic Party and its allies.

Let me pause for a moment, and tell the story of how the Koch Industries was born, how the Koch family made their billions and became the leading insurgents against the oil monopolies within the domestic United States. This story contains many lessons about the role of oil in the world economy.

Oil & the Rise of Russia

The father of the infamous Koch brothers was chemical engineer Fred Koch. In 1927 he invented a new method of thermal cracking, transforming crude oil into gasoline. The big oil bankers tried to put him out of business. They took him to court 44 different times. In one instance they were proven to have actually bribed the judge to rule against him.

Fred Koch was nearly ruined in the United States. The big oil men were not going to let him in on the business. But this was 1927, and there was another place for oil innovators to turn. Koch found himself invited to the Soviet Union.

Prior to the Bolshevik revolution, the Russian Empire had been one of the leading oil-exporting countries. 150 different oil companies were invested in the Baku oil fields in Azerbaijan, part of the Czarist empire. The foreign oil companies easily overpowered and controlled the local oil barons. Very few Russians made money from the empire's oil fields.

The biggest owners in the Baku oil fields were the Nobels, a Swedish family that owned an oil company. The French wing of the Rothschild banking dynasty had their own oil corporation, and they also owned a large amount of Baku oil. Both Nobel and the Rothschild oil corporations eventually merged into the megacorporation currently called Royal Dutch Shell.

Starting in 1898, the Baku petroleum output was larger than the entire domestic output of the United States. Half of the oil in the entire world was being produced in areas controlled by Russia.

Public control of oil and natural gas was key in transforming the Soviet Union into a world power during the 1930s.

As a result of its important role in the world economy, Baku was one of the few areas within the Russian Empire to have electricity. However, 95% of electricity was used for industrial purposes. The working peoples of Baku, half of them Turkish Muslims, the other half Christian Armenians, lived in shacks. They made poverty wages.

The peoples of the entire Russian Empire were living in extreme poverty. Russia was supplying the entire world, especially the mighty British Empire, with oil. Britain's victory in the First World War was won with tanks, airplanes, and military trucks powered by Russia's petroleum.

But the Russians, the Ukrainians, the Moldovans, the Azeris -- they didn't get any wealthier. Russia and the surrounding countries had backward agrarian economies. Mass starvation and malnutrition was routine.

A famous incident occurred in 1901. The Rothschilds banking family owned an oil refinery, located in Georgia, in the city of Batumi. The oil workers at this refinery went on strike demanding better conditions. The leaders of the oil workers union were arrested and taken to jail. So, in 1901, a crowd of thousands of Batumi oil workers, with guns blazing, ripped down the walls of the prison and freed their comrades. It made headlines all over the world.

The leader of the crowd that broke open the jails and freed the oil workers was a 23-year-old seminary school dropout. At the time he went by the nickname Koba. He would eventually be known to the world by the name Joseph Stalin.

Yes, the peoples of Russia and the surrounding countries knew it. They knew it in their bones that they were supplying the modern industrial economy of the 20th century with oil, making a lot of bankers rich, while they themselves were poor.

In the aftermath of the Russian Revolution of 1917, the British armed forces seized the oil fields of Baku. But over the course of the civil war, the Bolsheviks took them back. Lots and lots of blood was spilled in Baku and the rest of Azerbaijan. It was a hotly contested territory.

In the 1920s, most of the oil wells had been destroyed during the fighting. The Soviet government desperately needed oil production to get going again. Lots of foreign technicians and experts were brought in to help industrialize. Fred Koch came to Russia in 1929 to train Soviet oil technicians.

Fred Koch, an American oil chemist, watched as an agrarian, Third World country become a world industrial power in a few short years. Between 1928 and 1936 the Soviet Union became the biggest producer of steel in the entire world. The Soviet Union also produced more tractors than any other country in the world. Of course, oil production went through the roof. The entire country was lit up with electricity.

The huts of rural villages where Soviet peasants lived were replaced with modern apartment buildings. Running water was provided for the entire country as well. Illiteracy was wiped out.

This was the 1930s. The rest of planet was having a Great Depression. But with a planned economy, the Soviet Union was booming. It built skyscrapers, and the beautiful Moscow subways. The newly constructed university system trained the children of illiterate peasants to grow up and become the scientists who first conquered outer space.

No, the Soviet Union did not become the worker's paradise many of the global Marxist and communist movements expected it to be. It was not heaven on earth. It was a society that had many big problems, which eventually played a role in its destruction.

But what the Soviet Union did between 1928 and 1936 was go from being an impoverished country, controlled by Britain and France as almost a semicolony, to gaining the status of a superpower. This is what happens when a society takes control of its resources and its economy. This is what happens when nations and peoples pull together to resist economic domination, and begin to chart their own course.

It doesn't require Marxism-Leninism. It doesn't require Soviet-style command economies. It requires economic independence. It requires mobilization of people. It requires leadership that loves the homeland, not the international bankers and billionaires.

Fred Koch was horrified by what he saw. Today, Fred Koch's two children sit at the center of a coalition of low-level American capitalists, billionaires who feel they've been excluded from the club. Fred Koch's two sons certainly hate communism, socialism, cooperation, and solidarity with every bone in their body, despite the fact that the work of

Fred Koch as a chemist was essential in building the Soviet Union.

Saudi Oil Suicide and the CIA

In 2014, the high oil prices that had been engineered by US foreign policy came to a sharp and sudden end. Suddenly, without any warning or real market justification, the Kingdom of Saudi Arabia began putting oil on the international markets. Saudi Arabia started putting tens of millions of barrels of oil onto the market every day.

This huge influx of oil caused demand to decrease, and the price to drop. But the Saudi Kingdom did not stop. The Saudis continued putting petroleum onto the international markets, and expanding their oil production apparatus.

Even though they cannot afford it, the Saudis take out loans, and continue building an even bigger oil production apparatus. Saudi Arabia is losing money, going nearly bankrupt, but it keeps putting oil onto the markets.

The Kingdom of Saudi Arabia is a close ally of the United States, with its oil resources controlled by Wall Street bankers.

The crown prince, the son of King Salman, announces that Saudi Arabia is transitioning away from oil.

A policy of shifting away from oil might make sense in Venezuela or Russia, but not in Saudi Arabia. Saudi Arabia is a giant desert. The country has two things: sand and oil.

Since 2014 the oil price has been dropping. It's gotten below $30 per barrel.

Saudi Arabia is having huge internal problems. On January 1 of 2016, 47 people were beheaded. Many of them were dissidents, including the leading Shia Cleric Ayatollah Al-Nimr. Riots are going on. Oil workers are unemployed, starving, and rioting.

Why is this happening? Why would the Saudis bankrupt themselves? Why would they slit their own wrists?

You have to look deeper.

Since the 1940s, when US President Franklin Delano Roosevelt established relations with the House of Saud, the oil has never really belonged to the Saudis.

Aramco, the Saudi oil company, has always just been a middle man. Saudi oil is controlled exclusively by the Big Four. The US oil trust – BP, Shell, Chevron, and Exxon-Mobil -- have always dictated exactly what the Saudis do with their oil.

The Saudis now have the fourth-largest military budget of any country in the world, and they purchase their weapons exclusively from the United States.

The Saudis are not independent. Saudi Arabia is just an extension of the big oil bankers who run Wall Street.

Saudi Arabia is dropping the price of oil intentionally because their bosses are commanding them to do so. This is a strategy that was cooked up inside the Council on Foreign Relations.

The goal is to put Iran, Russia, and Venezuela out of business. It's to beat back the wave of independence around the world that was spawned by the high oil policies of the Bush years. The goal is also to put the Koch brothers, Sarah Palin, and their crew of new oil billionaires out of business.

The goal is to restore the monopoly of the oil bankers.

I was in Caracas during the December election, and I saw firsthand what the CIA, their Saudi puppets, and their Rockefeller overlords are doing to that country. I saw lines around the block for ATMs, for toilet paper, and for other supplies.

The victory of the Venezuelan opposition at the polls was a direct result of a relentless effort to cash-starve Bolivarian socialism.

Russia has been forced to cut its domestic budget by 10%. The state-owned oil money that stabilized Russia is being cut back. The hope is to weaken Putin.

The oil-price drop brought Iran to the negotiating table. It put Iran in a situation where it was willing to make huge concessions, and give up its peaceful nuclear energy program.

Meanwhile, the fracking billionaires in Oklahoma and Texas are hurting. Energy stocks are dropping lower than ever. BP has already bought up a few of the fracking firms.

Don't doubt for a moment that the oil-price drop is part of US foreign policy strategy. We even have a confession of sorts from the son of Ronald Reagan. Michael Reagan said:

"Since selling oil was the source of the Kremlin's wealth, my father got the Saudis to flood the market with cheap oil.

"Lower oil prices devalued the ruble, causing the USSR to go bankrupt, which led to perestroika and Mikhail Gorbachev and the collapse of the Soviet Empire."

Obama is now doing the same thing, according to Michael Reagan.

The oil-price drop of the 1980s also served political purposes, and it was also carried out by Saudi Arabia.

In the 1980s, the Soviet Union was reorienting its economy toward selling oil. France, West Germany, and other European countries announced that they were more open to purchasing Soviet oil.

The Soviet government launched a project to build the Urengoy pipeline, an oil pipeline also called the Trans-Siberian pipeline. This was a gigantic oil pipeline that connected the Siberian oil fields with Western Europe. The Soviet government invested billions of dollars in this project, expecting that in the 1980s they would be able to use this pipeline to sell oil to Europe.

After billions and billions of dollars had been spent by the Soviet government, the Saudis dropped the oil prices, the same way they are doing now. The pipeline was completed in 1984. Because of the oil-price drop, it never even paid for itself.

This was a large factor in the economic problems facing the Soviet Union in the 1980s, which led to perestroika and eventually the end of the Soviet government.

The Wal-Mart Computer Crash

Price manipulation, the artificial dropping and raising of commodity prices -- this is how John D. Rockefeller created Standard Oil, the corporation that is the direct ancestor of today's super-major called Exxon-Mobil. John D. Rockefeller became the master of what Americans now know very well as a Wal-Mart scheme.

The store called Wal-Mart in the United States has ruined the economies of thousands and thousands of cities and municipalities by setting up shop and lowering its prices. Wal-Mart starts selling TVs, radios and kitchen supplies at the lowest prices imaginable. That is, until all the other stores go out of business. Then, it raises the prices higher than ever, because it has a monopoly.

But the oil Wal-Mart scheme is getting out of control. The price of natural gas always follows right behind oil, and it's cheaper than ever. The price of copper and steel is dropping lower than ever also. Gold is low. Silver is low.

All the key commodities are losing value. Following right behind the oil drop, prices are dropping in almost every sector.

Meanwhile, Wal-Mart, the retail store that is biggest employer in the United States, is laying off people in droves. Stores are closing, because Americans cannot afford to keep buying the way they once did.

During the 1990s, Alan Greenspan legalized all kinds of predatory lending practices, allowing people to get ripoff credit card and housing loans. As the spending power of the US public decreased, the idea was to keep the economy going. They created an economy of rabid consumerism. They taught the people of the United States -- who had seen their standard of living rapidly decrease; who had lost their good-paying industrial jobs; who were paying tens of thousands of dollars just to go to college -- to spend money that they do not have, and temporarily prop up a decaying economy.

But Wal-Mart capitalism is failing. The American middle class is dead. The American dream, the house with the white picket fence has been foreclosed.

The oil-price drop has made gasoline cheaper than ever. But go to any gas station in the Midwest on any given day, and I can promise you will see a car pull up. It will have a mother in it, and one or maybe two children in the backseat.

She will pull up to the gas station, and she will reach very carefully for the gas pump, and she will very carefully stick it into her gas tank, and put $4 gas into her car.

Just four dollars of gas! Why? Because that's all she can afford. One dollar of gas can get her kids to school the next day. It can get her to work after that. It's just enough to keep going.

For a long time in the United States, the white workers and the billionaires had an understanding. It went like this: The billionaires got to go all over the world and slaughter people and murder people. They had coups in Latin America. They dropped bombs in Vietnam and Korea. They built a huge nuclear arsenal. They beat down, exploited and oppressed the African Americans and Latinos.

Government spending on warfare, policing agencies, and prisons has become essential to the US economy. The United States is gradually transitioning into a low-wage police state.

The deal was that, as long as the white workers went along with this, and didn't get in the way, and kept waving the flag and cheering for empire, they would get TV sets, cars, houses -- the so-called "American Dream." A high standard of living.

But this agreement was terminated. In the 1980s it started to gradually erode, and in 2016 it is completely gone. The white American middle class is suffering, civil liberties are disappearing, and the country is in an economic meltdown. Youth from the South and Midwest are fleeing to the coastal areas -- California, Manhattan, and New England -- because life has become unlivable in the once-prosperous industrial heartland.

The problem in the oil markets is just a reflection of a bigger problem. The computer revolution of the 1990s has made production so efficient. Decades ago they had book binderies. Hundreds and sometimes thousands of people would be employed in factories binding books. Today they have a machine that can be operated by a single person. Files are uploaded, a single button is pushed, and books come out.

The computer revolution has resulted in mass poverty for millions of people. Millions of people are starving, fleeing their homes, becoming migrants, because they no longer have a place at the assembly line. The global apparatus of production has become so efficient, that millions of people are not needed any longer. They no longer have a place at the assembly line.

Because they aren't being hired any longer, the millions of people cast out of production are not spending money. They are not purchasing the billions and billions of dollars worth of goods that are being so efficiently churned out.

A glut of overproduction is threatening the planet.

Millions of people in Africa and the Middle East, who are no longer profitable to the billionaires and capitalists, are packing themselves onto ships and fleeing to Europe. People in Southeast Asia, Indonesia, and the Philippines are spreading out all over the world. People in Mexico and Guatemala are fleeing to the United States in order to survive.

Everywhere there is a huge abundance of resources and products, but a shortage of jobs and livelihoods for the people.

"Accumulation through Destruction"

As my friend the brilliant economist Bill Dores has explained, capitalism has moved into a mode called "accumulation through destruction."

How did the United States become the unrivaled center of the world economy anyhow? After the Second World War, the rest of the world was destroyed.

The US economy is centered around war. It's a vulgar kind of Keynesianism. US corporations keep their profits rolling in by building bombs, tanks, drones, and other military hardware to kill people around the world.

The USA has a system of prisons for profit. Private corporations are paid to lock away people who break the law in prison. There is an economic incentive for high crime rates and for people to be locked in jail. The United States has the largest prison population in the entire world, because imprisoning people is a way to make money.

US President Franklin Roosevelt restricted the power of wealthy corporations. Under his leadership, the United States aligned with the Soviet Union in order to defeat fascism.

One of the biggest myths purported by the capitalists is this idea that markets create and unleash innovation. If you think the free market creates innovation, tell me: why does Hollywood make the same movie over and over and over again?

Yes, capitalists take risks, but they would prefer not to. They want the most secure investment possible. They want to maximize profits; they don't have any other purpose. Where did the computer revolution in technology come from? Many trace it back to the decoding machines constructed during the Second World War. This wasn't the innovation of private capitalists and the market.

During the war, Roosevelt sat down with the capitalists, and said, "We are going to defeat the Nazis." He said, "In order to defeat fascism, you must give up your economic freedom. You must function as a part of a team. You must obey the democratic government and work for the good of the country." The United States, the Soviet Union, Britain, and France did not defeat the Nazis by allowing corporations to make endless profits. NO!

During the war, even in the capitalist west, the corporations went under complete government management. They obeyed the president and the military. They coordinated everything for the defense of democracy. Some of the first computers were designed by smart people, hired by the government, and unleashed to invent and develop new methods for winning the war.

China has Broken Free

The media coming from the western world does not acknowledge the problem of capitalist over-production. No, western media commentators and economic analysts have a single, one-word answer about what is causing the problems of the global economy: China.

They don't explain how, or why, but somehow China is to blame. They say "China did it." They call it the "Chinese slowdown."

It's very important that we talk about what's actually going on in the Chinese economy, because it actually points to the way out of this insanity.

Back in the 1920s and 30s China was called the "sick man of Asia." A very large percentage of the population were drug addicts. The British had actually forced China to accept heroin and opium imports. The drugs allowed China to be economically crippled and enslaved.

Chinese President Xi Jinping is leading a massive crackdown on corruption, asserting that the overall success of Chinese society takes priority over corporate profits.

Parks in major Chinese cities were reserved for white Europeans. They famously had signs that said "No dogs or Chinese allowed." Imagine what it must have been like for Chinese people, a people with such a proud, beautiful history, to see signs like that put up within their homeland.

The western capitalists have completely re-written history. They tell us that Asia, and Africa, and Latin America, and the Middle East have always been poor. But this is a lie!

While my ancestors in Ireland and France were living in caves, people on this continent had vibrant civilizations, the Incas, the Aztecs, the Maya.

The Middle East was the cradle of civilization with Hammurabi, Mesopotamia, and Persepolis.

The African continent had Timbuktu and the Pyramids of Giza.

The western colonizers are not "civilizing" the peoples they have conquered. They are not "developing."

When the British Empire went to India, they saw the vast textile industry. They did not invest in it and develop it. They burned down the textile mills! They forced the people of India to buy their cloth from Britain.

In Mexico today, the farmers have been tossed off their land. They once grew their own food, but now they purchase it from US food corporations.

The imperialists don't want producers. They don't want nations and peoples to develop. They want captive consumers. They want to conquer markets, destroy production, and force everyone to purchase from them.

Long before 1949, the imperialists had been "investing" in China. They had been doing business there, but the Chinese people were poorer than they had ever been.

In 1949, this changed. A new government came into power. China had never had any steel production, but with assistance from the Soviet Union, China launched its steel industry in the 1950s.

China began to produce its own cotton, its own clothing. China built power plants and hospitals.

In 1961, the Soviet Union cut off its aid to China. China could not depend on Soviet assistance any longer. Briefly it attempted to be more egalitarian than the Soviet Union. During the Cultural Revolution, Mao Zedong, Lin Biao and the Gang of Four tried to move closer to a kind of utopian vision of communism.

In 1978, the policies shifted. Deng Xiaoping said, "To get rich is glorious." Many people see this statement as embracing capitalism. But it was the opposite. He said, "Poverty is anti-communist, but to get rich is glorious."

He said that China could not become a prosperous nation by redistributing poverty. Deng Xiaoping's vision of "Socialism with Chinese Characteristics" was based on raising the level of productive forces.

As China stepped back from the command economy, it started importing all kinds of western products, and allowing western capitalists to do business. Wall Street started making lots of money from China.

But at the same time that western corporations were investing in China, and selling Chinese products, the Chinese Communist Party was keeping a firm hand on things. Corporations had no freedom.

No other society in history has executed billionaires. But every Chinese business owner knows that if he gets on the wrong side of the Communist Party, he could be dead.

Recently, the owners of a McDonald's meat distributor in China, a US-based corporation called OSI, were caught distributing rotten meat to the public. The Communist Party leaders in Shanghai dragged them out of their offices in handcuffs. Executives from this wealthy US corporation have been put into prison.

So what is this Chinese slowdown? What does it have to do with the world economy?

China has stood up. What started in the mountains with Mao Zedong and the Eight Route Army has resulted in an entirely new situation for the whole country. China had no steel mills in 1949. Today, 50% of the world's steel is produced by China's government-owned and -controlled steel industry.

China makes its own cars, its own cell phones, its own satellites. The Chinese slowdown is the result of the fact that China is no longer buying things from the colonizers and imperialists. The Wall Street bankers cannot depend on making money from China, because China has stood up. It has its own independent economy.

Yes, there is a slowdown on the Chinese stock market, the vehicle created for western investment. But Chinese society is doing very well. The wages of the average Chinese worker have tripled since the dawn of the 21st century. In 2012, the wages of Chinese industrial workers increased by 14%.

Even CNN admits that almost every day another Chinese person becomes a millionaire. The world tourism industry is having a boom because there is now a wave of Chinese tourists. Chinese people whose grandparents were illiterate and lived as peasants serving landlords almost as property are going on vacations to Paris, the United States, and the tropical islands.

China has risen up out of centuries of degradation and poverty. Millions and millions and millions of Chinese people now have a lifestyle that many people in Africa, Asia, and Latin America can only imagine.

How did they do it? They did it by taking control of their economy.

Capitalism = Profits in Command

There's a lot of confusion about capitalism and socialism these days. Some people say China is capitalist, because it clearly doesn't have an economy like what existed in the Soviet Union.

Meanwhile, in the United States, Bernie Sanders is running for president saying he believes in socialism. When asked what socialism is, he says its means "a government that works for everyone." If this is all that socialism means, then every candidate should be called a "socialist." No candidate admits they want the government to function exclusively for an elite.

There is so much confusion.

What is capitalism? The best definition of capitalism I can find comes from Friedrich Engels, the close collaborator of Karl Marx. He explained what capitalism was by saying, "Under capitalism, the means of production only function as preliminary transformation into capital."

Capitalism is a system where houses don't get built because people need shelter. Under capitalism, houses are built so landlords and bankers can make money from selling and renting them.

Under capitalism, food isn't produced so that people can eat it. Food is produced so that capitalists can make money selling it.

Capitalism is a system where money gives the orders, and the rest of society follows behind the insanity of the market.

What is the alternative? You can call it "socialism," you can call it "people's power," you can call it "central planning" -- you can call it whatever you want.

The alternative is when rational human beings run the economy, and force it to function for the good of society.

In the world today, there is another kind of government that is emerging. It's a kind of government that derives its strength from community organizations, labor unions, and a mass involvement on the part of ordinary people in public affairs.

My friends here in Brazil, I tell you this carefully -- and I don't tell you this as an American, I tell you this as someone looking at the world and trying to make sense of it:

Don't give up Petrobas! Don't let Rockefeller, Carnegie, Du Pont, and Rothschild come into Brazil! Preserve your independence! Preserve your republic and domestic control of your natural resources!

Social movements of the working class are key to strengthening popular power and defeating capitalism.

If you want a strong prosperous country, you cannot hand over your economy to the Wall Street bankers. They function to destroy economies.

The brilliant man, a longtime activist in New York City who has travelled all over the world, and dedicated his life to fight for justice -- I mentioned him before, Bill Dores -- the man who taught me to think beyond politics to economics, if he has taught me anything, it is that Wall Street does not bring development. It does not seek to play fair on the world market. It wants to destroy any people or nation that rise up and start building themselves up. It wants people divided, poor, desperate, and dependent.

Fighting For a Better World

The forces of evil behind modern international capitalism have no loyalty of any kind. These capitalists aren't patriotic. They aren't religious. They don't worship any God but money. They blindly and fanatically worship their own profits, and they obediently follow wherever the crazed, irrational, invisible hand described by Adam Smith directs them to go.

I believe there is a deeper truth in the universe. I believe that right and wrong do exist. I believe that there is a higher purpose to life than simply a mad pursuit of money.

The only alternative to the insane greed that has seized the western world is popular power. The people must be in motion. They must be demanding justice and equality. They must stand arm in arm to fight for their rights. They must take control of the economies, and force them to function for public good.

The work that all of you are doing as labor leaders is essential.

I was particularly touched to be invited to a conference of labor leaders. When I was ten years old, living in rural Ohio, I was not thinking about politics. But my mother was a librarian.

Some of the librarians in her system were being harassed on the job. They wanted security. They met with the bosses and the bosses refused to provide it. So, as part of the Service Employees International Union, they went on strike.

As a ten-year-old child, I walked the picket lines, and learned the importance of class struggle. I learned never to cross a picket line, and that when working people stand together, great things can happen.

The particular library that my mother worked at was safe. They did not need security. But this did not matter to her and her co-workers. If their sisters walked out, they walked out with them. An injury to one is an injury to all!

This is worker's solidarity. This is the hope for the future of humanity.

Long live worker's solidarity!

Long live the CSB (Trade Union Center of Brazil)!

Long Live People's Power!

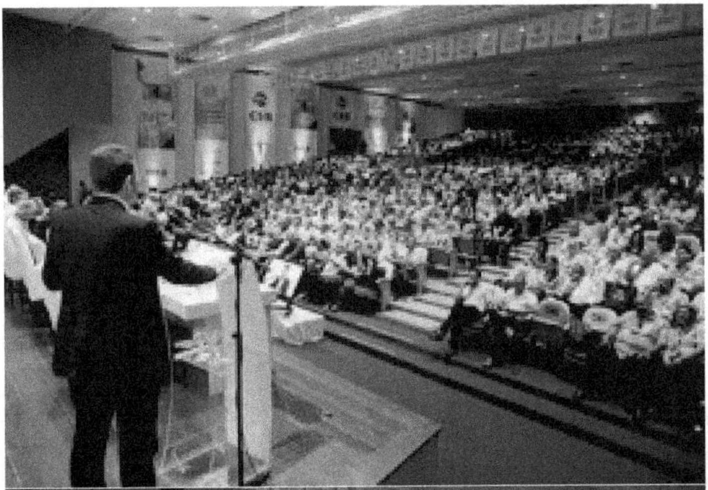
CSB

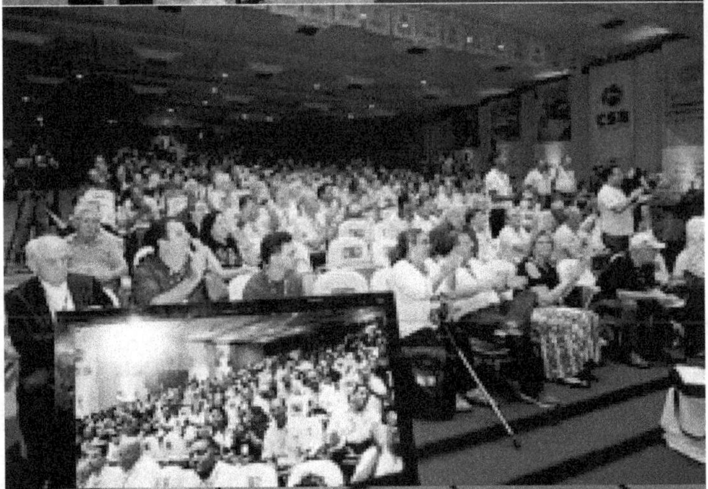
CSB

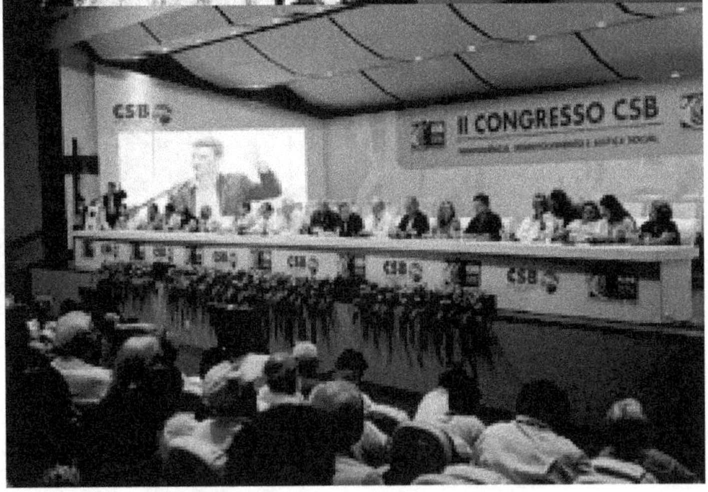
CSB
II CONGRESSO CSB
CSB

Above: Caleb Maupin with Antonio Neto, President of the Trade Union Center of Brazil (CSB)